Between the Crackups

REBECCA LEHMANN has an MFA from the Iowa Writers' Workshop, and a PhD in poetry and critical theory from Florida State University. She has been a Resident at the Millay Colony for the Arts, and the Vermont Studio Center. She lives in La Crosse, Wisconsin, USA, with her husband, where she teaches creative writing and literature.

Between the Crackups

REBECCA LEHMANN has an MFA from the Iowa Writers' Workshop, and a PhD in poetry and critical theory from Florida State University. She has been a Resident at the Millay Colony for the Arts, and the Vermont Studio Center. She lives in La Crosse, Wisconsin, USA, with her husband, where she teaches creative writing and literature.

Between the Crackups

REBECCA LEHMANN

SALT

LONDON

PUBLISHED BY SALT PUBLISHING

Acre House, 11–15 William Road, London NW1 3ER, United Kingdom

© Rebecca Lehmann 2011

The right of Rebecca Lehmann to be identified as the
author of this work has been asserted by her in accordance
with Section 77 of the Copyright, Designs and Patents Act 1988.

Salt Publishing 2011

Printed and bound in the United States by Lightning Source Inc.

Typeset in Swift 9.5 / 13

ISBN 978 1 84471 858 0 paperback

1 3 5 7 9 8 6 4 2

For Josh

Contents

III. THE POEM IS THE STORY

Acknowledgements

Grateful acknowledgement is made to the editors of the following publications, in which these poems first appeared, and to the Millay Colony for the Arts, and the Vermont Studio Center, where many of the poems in this manuscript were written.

Alaska Quarterly Review: "One Hundred Words For Loser"
Best New Poets 2010, and *Contrary*: "The Factory: An Elegy In Six Parts"
The Canary: "The Devil Is In Detroit"
Columbia Poetry Review: "To Feed And Water Ourselves And Others"
Conduit: "$1/\infty=0$"
Connotations: "A Gun In The First Act"
Denver Quarterly: "Ten Bells Tell," "Lands End"
Drunken Boat: "A Dream Of The Rood (1)," "A Dream Of The Rood (2)"
Forklift Ohio: "Someone Has Sent A Letter," "Look At The Trees"
The Gettysburg Review: "Under Vision Walls," "The End Of The World," "Has Anyone Seen Autumn," "Something Very Woman," "Year, Years A-Sparkle"
Hayden's Ferry Review: "The Youngest Girls In Memphis"
Indiana Review: "Bucolic Calling"
The Iowa Review: "The History of Yesterday," "Particulate Matter" (parts I, III & IV)
Makeout Creek: "The New Town Is Really The Old Town"
Narrative Magazine: "The Poem is the Story (1)," "The Poem is the Story (2)," "The Poem is the Story (3)," "The Poem is the Story (4)," "The Poem is the Story (5)," "North Florida Rain"
Or: "Pterodactyl Eye Chart," "Pasture"
Tin House: "Letters To A Shithead Friend"

Between the Crackups

I. The Devil Is In Detroit

A Hundred Words For Loser

Dear glove-puppet, you should come here;
it's grey and everybody hates you. A man
tells a bible story about a town filled
with prostitutes and a father who sleeps
with his two daughters. Their syphilitic shadows
slink across the ceiling tiles. And who cares
about the movements of their hidden girly ribbons?
They collect, but, don't worry; they stink

of sulfur and twist. In the back alley: half
a bologna sandwich, a flattened refrigerator box,
a hundred words for loser. You finger the rat's nest
at the base of my skull. Some suitor you are —
hey pussyfoot, hey horn-ball. Hey stupid,
bring me dead things and a flat stomach.

Letters To A Shithead Friend

Dear Friend,

I broke a glass this morning, and it reminded me of you, sprawled across the kitchen tiles. I've been keeping this news for a year and a half—my neighbor rifles through my garbage cans at night, and I sleep with a rusted scissors beneath my pillow. You want the truth?—mostly I am writing angry poems, hoping your teeth will fall out.

Dear Friend,

Sky blue is a stupid color. I don't care what burlesque girls have to do with ping-pong balls, you're still a shithead. I put a magnet over your face on the picture of us at the Lion's Hall dance on my fridge. Your attempt at communicating with me via crossword puzzle is lame. I'm sure you can think of something better than that, like skywriting or a parade of circus elephants.

Dear Friend,

I received the bouquet of balloons and have already popped them all. My long needle for sewing leather purses worked best for that. I draped the broken rubber parts over my houseplants and sang Happy Birthday to myself while chain smoking unfiltered cigarettes.

P.S. I can't understand you when you talk with your fingers in your mouth.

Dear Friend,

The ten kittens did not impress. I let them loose around the neighborhood, and got complaints. Now I have to go to a neighborhood coalition meeting and explain the whole situation to them, about the failed skywriting, and what a total shithead you are, and how I Magic-Marker all over your letters and send them to the children's wing of the local hospital to cheer up the cancer patients.

Dear Friend,

Please stop. I got sick off the cotton candy at the county fair I went to with the tickets you sent me. Let's face the golden clothed trumpeters; you're not going to win me over like this. I am tired of being angry. Not lions nor zebras nor cobras nor mongooses. No soda fountains. I can't touch your new jacket—don't mail it.

Dear Friend,

I have been in touch with an old lover. He has propositioned me. *I don't have an apology,* he said. He said, *I would have moved to Iowa with you if I had known about the tornados.* He is driving a motorbike here posthaste. He said, *Sidecar, tomato, bulgur-wheat, bumblebee.* I've picked up aviator glasses and a leather dolly. Good luck finding me ocean-side.

Dear Friend,

Your perseverance is stupid, because I don't like you anymore. I was just telling my dentist about the peppermints you left lining my porch railing. Luckily, they did not rot my teeth because I fed them to the local roosters. My old lover and I are building a boat to sail to Cuba. I am a tiny communist with sunburned shoulders. We are leaving our apologia under the southernmost boulder.

Comrade,

I have joined the ballet. Water from the secret *piscina* baptizes my esophagus. I am cleaner than you.

Dear Friend,

I can't express how much anger I feel towards you. After my stag leaps through the open-air courtyard, my record-breaking pike jumps off the rusty box spring of the used bed my old lover bought me. Let alone the frustration for getting me kicked out of Cuba. Back off. I left you a roll of pennies to throw at the pigeons by the fountain, so go use them. My watercolor class meets in an hour and I don't have time to stroll the boardwalk backwards with you.

P.S. My lazy eye will always watch the plum dish—don't even think about it.

Bucolic Calling

These were the times to fear. We were already falling. And had been. What we wanted were purple slugs, a slime to sing to. Give us the pretty girls, the pretty boys, the little child dead and mossy at the bottom of the well. Our hands against the stones were pounding, were pounding and bloody palmed. Look at us, at the bottom of the false wooden bottom, playing a joke on Mom. Look at her face, twisted with terror. But such was the age of us. We with our sunburned cheeks, with our frostbitten toes. We didn't care if they fell off. We wanted them to. We begged for it: *Please, please, God of the Toes, take ours as sacrifice and bring us a field of moist corn stalks and pig shit.* In the apple orchard the sticks stung like meanies. We unzipped ourselves and climbed the stout trunks. I had an apple in my hand and it was bruising as I threw it, the air pushing its skin in. Yours was a rotten one, already bruised and flying apart in the apple leaves, depositing its brown and mushy flesh in splatters. This was the way we came and Mom was in the gravel road crying and we laughed at her. We laughed and we laughed at her silly poor-person jacket and we laughed at her face, and at her silly tears.

The Youngest Girls In Memphis

The youngest girls in Memphis
wear bridal veils to afternoon tea.
They wake up from naps with double
vision and balled feet. We call them
brats, and mean it. They are all
too bold. At night, they drive hail-
dented cars across the fog-laced
highways of southern Tennessee.
They gulp cans of cherry pop. They sing
Heartbreak Hotel in falsetto, and smoke
in the airport lounge, although
they are travelling nowhere, and fast.

One day we notice their boots
have cut into their toes. Their feet
are bleeding. One day we notice
their eyes losing pressure, the filmy
sheen of glaucoma dressing
their pupils. They hang garlands
above their doorways, mark
an X in ash on each of ours. But,
they are just girls, after all,
we shouldn't expect too much.
Though their lips may purple
and peel, though their ears bleed

with the pain of the South,
though they are waxen
and unruly, still we want them
to sit at our breakfast nooks,
braiding one another's hair. Still we
want them to sing in soft coos
to our infants. We never expect them
to erupt like angered volcanoes,

their vomit and loose teeth pooling
on our tabletops. This is a surprise
every time; this is the event horizon.

To Feed And Water Ourselves And Others

Genesis as another word
for water on the knee.
As in, Exegesis motherfucker.
In combination we
moved like ducklings
trailing a honking line of traffic.

In hindsight, all ribbons
curled roundly. In retrospect.
Vision checked as 20/25.
You are my twine-sign,
my only twine-sign.

Left the jokes. We didn't mean them.
The color wheel sloppy.
The motor oil. Motor mouth.
Meet my left hand, it's
an open book. It's Miss Michigan.
It'll do the trick. Eyes closed.
Head tilted back. Fish pose.
The bandage finds your children,
floating in the hot tub.

We were writing their lessons
in the other room. On the hot roof,
hot tar and pigeons, clawing
a plastic bag open. Your husband and mother.
The food on the floor collecting
in a pile. The feeling of relief.
The feeling of relief. The need for glasses.

The End Of The World

An idea devolves before our eyes and no one
        takes the time to do anything personal about it—
        like your graveled voice.
My nature is to be very quiet.

The bonfire: the rain sizzled the burning logs.
No further comment is necessary.
I wanted to sing a song that had emotional register.

My nature changed; I broke out in a tan.
There's a place I'd like to visit; is it a mouth or a volcano?
I have a frontal lobe named Fuck You.

I've reached the end of the world; it's a whitewashed room.
I am by nature the kind of person who breaks down.
I didn't mean to touch your arm.

Drawn to the night sky, we clamored.
I wanted to ask you a question, but didn't want the answer.

Dusk became a mild return: a hike through
        the overgrown meadows.
The film-noir fog misplaced our steps,
        turned distance into blindness.

A man falls backwards from a second story window.
The man is you.

Muster Lovely

Dear tape measure, measure of what I'm doing
right now. Of my guilt, long and obsidian.

Dear front row seat. Dear brow, now furrowed,
I'm crowing, a cornet sounding off corporally.

Hear *Taps*, or *Anchors Away*. I will,
like the bird, lonesome and cold, drop

in a threesome onto a muck-skimmed pond.
How ethereal. How Pepsi-dark. How, like a lark,

I sing in self defeat, I crane away from
small matters. I blather and burst, a full

bladder of helium, or hope. Nothing matters,
I glide and respond, pound down and ground,

[like the grown man who apologized for calling
me a finger-fuck slut when we were both thirteen]

an amoeba, a game of tag, a hoard of children
screaming in the summer dusk.

Pterodactyl Eye Chart

Nothing but the chicken-talk
of old people, trying to make some
money. The butcher knife through
the heart of garlic, perched on
the cutting board. Needle point,
needle point, they are coming
to get us. We shiver in
the closet, hiding from the hard
hands. In the other town, the half-
child, we are waiting to hear
from _____, who is
renowned for conversational skills
and mousse-making ability. What a
tragedy to not find the answers, to find
the not answers we all don't have.
Watch us bend backwards with ease.
Watch us moon God. Our wrists are
detachable. Our moustaches
come off at night. We glow
in the stratosphere, finally exploding
in all our glory and trochees. We are
sprouting daisy petals, we are
the lost Pterodactyl.

And you, humming the song, humming
the commercial jingle, dreaming of reduced price hardware.

My Father's Fourth Tooth

My father's fourth tooth, then,
pulled and rotten to the root,

dropped in the bottom of a plastic bag.
Traces of blood stick to it;

it's clammy, a calamity. He's wan.
It's the first day of spring.

Let's reveal our darkest thoughts.
Where's the asparagus?

Behind the pine. It's not in season yet.
I was too busy picking my money

up off the ground to notice.
And there's the rare comet

we've all been waiting for, trailing
its frozen curtain. A fox hunches

on a bridge, cracking open a clam.
How pink its shell's ridges; how mealy

its muscle, its one lonesome tongue.
And the fox—his teeth gleaming,

his fur soaked with brackish water,
gray as my father's hair.

The Factory, An Elegy In Six Parts

1. THE MANAGERS

The Managers are giving silver dollars to our children,
are telling them that if they are good, they can have our jobs
once we've died. Inside the Factory we step on the steel
grating of the stairs tenuously, we operate with levers
and cogs, with finger-stained red buttons that read:
Push here in case of emergency. We dream of pitch blue sunsets
at night, of our children skipping ropes woven from reed-
grass in the center of a deserted parking lot. All their feet
lifting at the same time, all their reed ropes whooshing
against the pristine concrete, the silver dollars flipping
in their pockets—one coin per pocket, one pocket per child.

2. Call And Response

Manager: The motor smoked and tilted, unexpectedly.

Me: I sat on the chinked-metal mat and broke the socket wrench.

Manager: The conveyor belt twisted out of shape.

Me: The long ditch grass where your feet step.
In the factory, in the darkness, I am wondering how to name
the next passage of time.

Manager: Iridescent and beating to get to you.

Me: Even at this hour when the pavement has cooled.
None of my thoughts powerful, none moved the leaf flow.

Manager: I have given you the warning.

Me: The rest of the clunky machinery slid
through my fingers: my summer slip,
the red rose necklace, the two horse hitch.

Afterword: It's my own headache, caught up with me.
That's what the Managers tell me,
shaking their fists over fuck-wit fires.

3. Managerial Meeting

Factory A:
Output as maximal. No kerchiefs. No hazing.
No vending of hotdogs on Factory grounds.
Manufacture of: Holiday napkins, paper towel,
toilet paper (ass wipe — chortle, chortle), cocktail
napkins, scented and colored toilet paper (chortle —
ass wipe), Fourth of Juuuu-ly red-white-&-blue
napkins and paper towels with firework imprint
patterns, disposable paper bibs with front pockets
to catch spilled food from baby's mouth.

Factory B:
Output as efficient. More levers needed and
conveyor belt 11847c in need of repair. Gum
banned on Factory grounds. Manufacture of:
paper hospital gowns, paper booties, tampons
and sanitary napkins (cunt rags — chortle, chortle),
disposable diapers, paper coffee filters, sterile
paper hospital sheets, paper targets for shooting
ranges in shape of deer heads, paper targets for
shooting ranges in shape of human torsos,
disposable paper drinking cups with butterfly
pattern or alternate space ship pattern for boys.

Summation:
Calculation of losses: tax deductible and plashing.
Calculation of net gains: calculation compromised
by faulty abacus and lack of accurate statistics.
Calculation of employee breast size: adequate
(chortle, chortle).

4. Randall's Lament

Funny the colors that flow from our mouths,
quaking and pressed to the whitewashed walls.
The Managers all on balconies parading.
Dear Beatrice, I cannot feel your hand
in mine any more. Please send word if you are
still all okay. Found a bundle of toothpicks
under the machine from Todd's bad habit
of chewing them and spitting them.
Now Todd is being reprimanded. Polish
the gleaming metal until it says I love you.
Ammonia as a hard-strung savior. Dear Beatrice,
The children paraded past the window
this morning. Where are you now?
Todd is missing a tooth. The way to salvation
to admit guilt and culpability. So say
the Managers, all mighty and around us.
They are all sparkling and laughing
in their white coats and shined shoes. I think
they must be made of the dust of the universe,
the very best dust of the very biggest bang.

Beatrice's reply: Dear Randall, I am a cadet
in red and am all day feeling like swimming
in the pulp vats. And yesterday a man
was fished out like nothing, drowned.
Our Managers are also a-sparkle. Wave
to the children when they pass the next time,
and remember I am only six times six.

5. A Trial Is A Way To Find Guilt

Find me wicked or don't.
As the solution to a problem,
with streamers. At the old
park, the stranger on the car's
hood, the bloated water tower,
bold black letters spelling
the Factory's name. The teenagers
ready to take my place, eager,
and some in suits, and some
in coveralls. The noose. The pine-
cones and puffball mushrooms
arranged as a crown. The squirrels
watching from the oaks. If I say,
This is what we were, the Managers
respond, So be it. The switch
on my back and on your back.

If I say, Mercy, the Managers
respond, Let the worker
swing from the neck until dead
or bluing. The grass bulging
fingers reaching for my feet.
The sky like a bathtub
emptying, the sun a glob
of blond hair clogging its drain.

6. Memo To All Workers

If we, Managers, supervise the crease machine.
If you, workers, operate on multiple levels.
If kerchiefs are banned on Factory grounds.
If each conveyor belt ticks along smoothly.
If there is no incident of ruckus among you.
If the windows are blackened. If the windows
are opened. If air conditioning is installed.
You will not mention Todd or toothpicks.
You will not mention Beatrice and Randall.
You will not cover your breasts with baggy
T-shirts any longer but will wear requisite
uniforms without complaint, unless you are
men, and then T-shirts are okay for now.
You will not mention the park. Your children
marching past the windows every morning
and afternoon, the sight of their cuffed
socks and saddle shoes. You will not steal
sanitary napkins from the cunt rag production
area of Factory B. You will hum the national
anthem while you work. On key. Not in F,
but in F sharp because sharps are happy.
You will wear work gloves when necessary.
You will tell us, the Managers, that we look
very nice when we are supervising your work
or walking on the balconies above you.
You will not get headaches. You will not
get headaches. You will not get headaches.
You will practice reverence, and it will flood
you like coolant, like the river below the Factory,
overflowing with rain, covering your former homes.

The Devil Is In Detroit

For instance, you fucked me with my feet
up by my head, but never gathered me to you.
Often, when you fucked me from behind,
you imagined I was a man. When I was on top
you imagined I was younger. You wanted my breasts
to be perkier. You wanted me to get rid of my moustache.
When you did fuck me and you were on top,
you imagined I was a doll, with ringlets in ribbons.
Put this pink smock on, you said once,
and, *The Devil is in Detroit*. He must have been
riding in a Cadillac. I'll never forget
what your limp penis looked like in the bathtub,
a wet puppy nestled in your testicles. You didn't
like disturbance. I put my feet in anyway.
You put your hands on my face,
like this, and they left a mark. You put
your hands above my heart, like this, and pushed,
1, 2, 3. I didn't know what you thought
when you fucked me while I slept. I was
asleep then; I could only smell you.
If saffron could come like that, clinging tightly
to my buttocks, then surely you could too.
With your puffed up fuck fingers
you left red welts on my fanny,
flopped your penis back and forth before it hardened.

When you were fucking her, you were looking down
at her tiny teacups jiggling up and sideways.
You slapped her forehead. You slapped her throat.
The birds outside the windows chirped,
the curtains blew across your back.
You could hear me moving through the floor.
You called her Bully, pushed in harder.
Between the crackups, a light came,
strong enough to cut the blight.

I had my legs open, like I was.
The air filled, the smell of hot plastic cups
and sickbed. And tissue. And if you could
have touched me there, you did.
I never told anyone the bruise you made,
but wished I had a bone to break against the wood.

II. Think Georgia, Gorgeous

My Mister's Eyes

My mister's eyes are floating tubs of rum.
Corralled, more or less resting, he lisps dread.
He snorkels wide, then he brings me home.
He has been wary. Blood whips groans, he read,
always seven groans, damasked, reddened slight.
Unanswered, he grows the sea. He reeks.
He ends simple fumes, a thread more light,
then into better form my mister shrieks.

All terror peaks. You'll tell, I know.
My muse charts after more, pleads, swings round,
un-granting ever awe. A god does go.
My mister when he wails drags on the ground.
And yet, he's heaving, my tongue-stunned love.
I see him. He scrapes the fulsome air.

A Dream Of The Rood

As in the dream I had last night, I found a baby in a cardboard box, and a port-o-potty spilled a flood of shit and half-dissolved toilet paper on my legs. I had an old lacquered high-chair and a wooden hairbrush. And you were there, and you, and even you. I wrote my gospel on a post-it: Help me with my handstand. Cushion my nether-region, my falling party-favor, I like the duck, duck   goose. As in how lilies taste like bitter religion. As in my tongue on the oak tree's trunk, on the rigid bark, feeling for devil-worms. Nevertheless, not the tree of victory. Not the hollyhock. Not the last bleat of the lonesome goat. We are all thrumming from within our fatty lobes. The death warrant arrived via prosopopoeiac vision. The Man with his list of who behaved this way, and who behaved that way. He asked me if I was a Catholic, and I couldn't answer yes. He waved a signal in my face, a beacon, and I shuddered to think of the loop-hole, of the compact, burning punishment. Of the way dry-rotted barn beams tremble and bend.

A Dream Of The Rood

As in the dream I had last night, my old mechanic was elected president, and we fucked on a weight bench until my triceps throbbed and buckled. If I have five jewels, they are imbedded in my breastbone. The wood is sweating. I am sweating. Then we chased the vision of the babbling sequoia. However it was bleeding—it ripped the sky open. There is the fancy mead-hall table with God and Jesus and all-saints. There is the plump turkey leg. There is a shinier version of myself, all wrapped around with gold and silver garments. And so the Man and his right hand. And so the filth-bearing owl. And so a tree above all other trees. For then once a man asked me to marry him in a rotted-out redwood trunk. Then we drank wine and rubbed the dusky walls with our backs. If I have four corners they are spread thinly. If I have a foot in each dimension, I am doing the galactic splits. If, in the night, the tree stalks me, I will bear witness to its maleficent greed, to its splintered breath and carnal haste.

Think Georgia, Gorgeous

We take our bearings from the headlights
flashing through the guardrails. Nashville,
and a billboard reads, *Good little tits!* No,
that's a joke you make. But we saw one
in Indiana that read *Fireworks, Guns, Cigarettes,
Big B-A-N-G!* Tennessee's small towns rub
themselves against our little Chevy as we careen
through the Smokies. I grab the wheel when
you ask me to, put down my pencil and stop
following the law. The truth collapses. There's
a mountain that looks like your face. I say
I love you. It's not a lie, although everything else
might be—the salt on the side of the car,
the salt in your blood, the one-armed hitchhiker.

Ten Bells Tell

Visions of lovebirds and prickled pears,
an inability to spell or tell
time, a heightened sense of hearing,

as in to hear the little tweets
upon the grates.
Had they but singsong
equal to their greeting.

To hear ten bells tells
we are falling, the bruise
on the leg like an angered owl.
The fingers peeling back,
weird human tricks, in the palm
a scar the shape of a supernova.
A pocketknife cut through.

Inability to hold one's head up.
To hear ten bells tells
we are not dying after all.

We may believe we are.
One's hands like jackrabbits
ready to hop and bite
the nipples of one's lover.
One's head in silhouette.
In the maelstrom. And all the birds.

To hear the tin cups.
The ten-tin-cupping-nation
of the bells, bells, bells.
Not signaling apocalypse.

To scar the face. An inability
to hold one's head at bay.
On the offensive, the pungent
smell of body in a Southern summer.
The odor like rotting cacti
and cat piss. The weather a crash.

The face in place. To cut
the hands. To pull the skin
back, spit in the wound.

Inability to bifurcate during times
of stress and resolute paranoia.
Inability to stay within one's shoes.
Cover up the face with a scarf
like winter. The stink. Inability,
the hard-song. The coming together.

The New Town

To find our new home in a new town newly inhabited by our new friends.
To stay in the motel past check out time, our limbs heavy as death.
In the new town the sheen of light off the frozen bay.
Through our new kitchen window the sheen blinds our curious eyes.
What we've got: a nearby park, a sidewalk, a pull-out bed.
What we lack: ice skates, proper outerwear, the correct regional accents.
And other people are adapting all along the snowy landscape.
You, in the bed beside me, soft, your breath like a child's hand on my neck.
The cold air a legion of ice picks stunting my lungs.

The new town is really the old town, turned leftward one degree and vibrating.
The frozen sheen is a cheetah made of light; it will catch us, if we run.

Front Yard Regatta

The yard fills up with weft and wire,
with the feather-some jay. The days, too hot
and expensive: each trip to the gas station,
each fumble of the pump, the gasoline
a lazy dribble. Every hour a new desire
for knowledge. Which months are good
for oysters? Which herbs cause diarrhea?
The bruised humidity of the late afternoon
ushers in a litany of silt and cockroaches.

How many evenings are spent praying
for flotillas? Wayward letters clutter
mailboxes. Bedraggled cats cast themselves
as strays in the drainage pipes. Their low moans
skidder to a halt, and heft, and harrow.

Let's Go To The Party

You have your sad boy mask on again.
It's afternoon, the sky splits. The scar
on your arm is a Carmen Figuratum;
that's a headache. Or an eye sore.
But the idle of the car, then its backing
out of the driveway, that's *adios amigos*.
I left my kaleidoscope on a park bench.
You were in the library reading *Les Misérables*.

Only I read it first. Only you say I stole
your copy to read it first. Maybe we both read it
in Islamorada on Spring Break three years ago.
One tequila, two tequila, three tequila—
a song I forget, like the shiny Canadian quarter
I dropped to the bottom of my glass of beer.

One Morning I Wake Up

One morning I wake up and everything is darkling
      (I listen).
One morning it's all light. I get stuck in the bathtub.
The cicadas churl on the other side of the window screen.

I have seen the chartreuse neologian.
I have seen his wailing eyes.

But an egg is the only thing I see when I close my eyes.
A man dressed in purple balances it on a countertop.
It's the equinox; the egg is perfectly poised.

No, it's summer.
It's I've-got-my-glasses-on-and-now-I-can-see-you.
It's go-to-sleep-now.

Somewhere a man is closing a door,
      which is not the door to my subconscious;
      it is the door to yours.

Listen, it's time for a chimney.
It's time for a face carved into an apple.

I want to place sprigs of lavender in the folded up bed sheets.
It will look like the miracle your hands make:
      the uncomfortable slice of bathing suit elastic on my skin,
      removed.
Or, the cold planks of the wood floor on naked feet.

Lands End

If lovers meet where lands end,
scattershot and alone. If I remind
my father of his mother, long dead.
If the year changes and autumn
never comes. If I can't leave
the South fast enough. If homeliness
is a way of life. If I want to put
my heart against a blank white wall.
If a hurricane. Even so,

the insistence of proximity.
If the flea market, crowded with
vendors and the big electric fans
stirring the dirt floor up
in billows, not really cooling.
The man with the thick drawl selling
cast iron pans and paperbacks.
If my father was a carpenter
for many years, then wasn't.
If my mother is a loose slip
hanging from a doorknob
in the morning. If I have brothers,
or not. If the line of my consciousness
was pistol whipped. If purpled.

If my father said to my mother,
I have a box filled with presents
for you. If the box is made
of wood from the old shed.
If my mother is a rope swing,
tied in knots and fraying.
My foot rests in the noose
of her neck. If I've mis-
behaved. At land's end.

My arm a leaden knocker. If my
recitation, then:

I'm just a poor girl,
from a poor family. Scaramouche,
Scaramouche, will you do the fandango?

Something Very Woman

Get a gander — it's the sun.
Don't stare too long.
What's left of the day?
That's my grandiose heart.

Your ideal version of yourself would be
        capable of participation.
The rain refused to stop.
Between the rain and the sun, go stand there.
You will radiate light.

In the morning you moved wood off the road.
Can you hear the sound?
The roar?
      It means break a window.

I couldn't go in the room once you'd left.
It was empty and looked as though you'd never been there.

I was supposed to be someone else.
I packed my bag.
Why should anything be inappropriate?
Or nothing?

And when I wiped the toothpaste from
        your mouth, it meant I wanted you.
Are you flushed?
I've thinned.

In the morning my throat hurt.
My feet were cut.
I woke up and hefted a sob.
You left your _____ in the room, and nothing else.

$1/\infty=0$

The equation of our lives is expressed
as a measure of something—
we just can't remember what.
Perhaps it is something easy,
like sleep or joy. The peeling
laminate of the shower wall
would not qualify. Or maybe it would,
if, underneath the cheap plastic,
between the mold-bloated studs,
there were something truly beautiful.
Maybe there's a basket of kittens,
certainly not dead and maggot ridden—
maybe an old library book, a smudged
due-date stamped in red on the ivory card
tucked inside its paper pocket.

The morning that I found out
the man I'd once wanted to marry
was marrying someone else was like
a sheet of black construction paper.
I thought about the bigness of the universe,
about the astronomy professor I had
in college who presented the class
with an impossible equation
to track the speed of a star
exponentially moving away from us
in the expanding ether of space
(imagine the universe like plum pudding,
the textbook read, in which the plums
represent stars; as the pudding bakes,
the plums move farther
and farther away from each other).

I couldn't solve the problem,
only made it as far as $1/\infty=0$.

The terror that brought. Later,
that night, I woke from a dream
I'd had of a snarling monster
nesting in my oven, its matted fur
spotted with light and ice, its snaggle-
tooth a mess of old skulls, forced together.

North Florida Rain

Don't judge me because I don't find anything as beautiful
as the sound of the rain; it's likely I've mistaken
anesthesia for aesthetics. Live oaks split the air around
my house. They don't know the answer: moonshine
or memory, perhaps trying to see each twisting drop amidst
the rapid veil. Years ago a deer ran out from the storm-slick
woods and slammed into the side of my car. The deer's antlers
slid across the windshield. Its hoofs dented lines across
the hood. Its nose was snotty. It snorted. A wad of mucus
lodged against the wipers. The ditch was something final.

Maybe the deer became the rain as it limped away,
the line of blood it left a lightning bolt, or question mark.
Forgive the intrusion of metaphor; I've been away a long time.
I wear a damp wool coat. Please page my father.

Look At The Tree

Look at the tree, at its top, filled out with dirty white blossoms.
There's a garden, and in it there are children.
They spin their toys in circles, like eyes.

Be forewarned, a porcupine will snarl, then rain will bring calamity.
The movement—we're hot, we're overheating.
Seven o'clock and we're awake.

On the old globe, Germany's de-militarized zone is shaded pink.
There's music, but it's rushing.

And what of the fathomless five?
Left at the border of "Hello" and "Come in, come in,
        I've been waiting for you."
This is how to rub a rose.
You shift on your feet.

Dye my shoes to match my dress, color me in.
Take two lefts and a right.

And then, you can't fathom this much.
Ants march across the driveway, each step an accusation.

Clarity—we were looking in an old shed window for it.
It was speckled with soot.
The dogwood branch, not the dogwood tree.

Sound is the answer to the question.
I made you on the corner.

III. The Poem Is The Story

A Gun In The First Act

Remember anger, barking fists. My knuckle rips open,
and we're nothing but an accident. The hard summer wind
holds itself back with strings. What is a leaf bug?
Before we can find one somebody drops a beer bottle;
it slurs across the gravel. We blame the night sky
for not coming fast enough, and with neon stars.
I was born in this puny city's tallest building. Gravity,
like rough forceps, sucked my fat head into the air.

The sky's a shiner. It moans. Short list: your heart, a handful
of muscle relaxants. We might be whale song, and not
even know it; that's why I wear rings. One morning I wake up
and find a Derringer, politely pearled, in the front yard.
Isn't this the mystery you were looking for? Dear Reader,
If I betray you, don't shoot me in the mouth.

Someone Has Sent A Letter

Someone has sent a letter and someone has returned a letter.
We were hanging out on the porch when it happened.
Suddenly an astute observer ambled over.
An armadillo was under the house, again.

But the house was on lifts so water could run under it.
The hour was blue or purple.
The house was whitewashed like a postcard picture of Greece.

And did you know, elephants can cry real tears?
The almonds extracted themselves from the air.
We were on sixes, or elevens.

Then it was night, then you got home from work,
then we were sleeping.
Except we weren't.

Expect this; it will all become a bypass.
One night it snowed in Florida but we slept through it.
Tomorrow we will drive to the Gulf of Mexico,
        but nobody will be there to see it.

Year, Years A-Sparkle

A little girl travelled with me by car to Poughkeepsie.
She asked if I had seen her purple heart.
She asked if I could see her.
She put the heart over her eye.

I thumbed the absence of memory; it smelled like oranges.
Your inaccessible nature reveals your humanity.
I wasn't permitted to say goodbye.

And it was like there were wires beneath our skin.
How can I blame you for wanting to leave quickly?

I said no I hadn't and I couldn't.
The diagonal line of bruises on the back
of my left thigh reveals my humanity.
Here's a joke: I don't get it.

The things one overhears: someone else's body
in the shower in the mornings.
The bathmat took on the smell of feet.
Yes, but only with my glasses on.

Please do something to make me laugh so I forget
how possible sadness is.
At the airport, I immerse myself in the din.
I blend in.

What is the sound of vacuous panic like?
I already have a statuette to represent that abstraction.
Don't combust until you see the whites of my eyes.

Dear Mr. _____, Would that I had met you once before.
I have allowed you use of my nail clippers and shampoo.
Please tell me about your mother's facial features.

In the doorway, in the morning, your silhouette against
        the sunlight, and then—
            you'd always been going to go.

Under Vision Walls

Think about desire.
A knife dropped down from the top of the ladder;
    we called it irony.

The cut on my scalp turned a clump of my hair pink.
A fingerprint, dried brown blood, stamped
    the white coffee mug.
That look, stop it.

The weather wavered.
One bickers, one feels the need to always be right.
Four answers to the question is there a god:
    clavicle, juniper, possibly, blossoms.

Beware the dingle, its leftward leaning light.
Do I feel like a fever?
The bruises on my legs, desire them.
To be scapular is to reach out.

I'd show you but I'm in a dress.
The chewing gum took some of the nausea away.
Is this loneliness?
Do you remember?

The footprints on the carpet — soot, black and persistent.
The horizon is a particular kind of mystery.
I had this idea to relate everything.

In the attic, the thunderstorm shook the rafters.
The whole house smelled like cedar.
You are very tall.

Dear Cousin

                              Death is a white
polar bear who visits me in dreams.
He runs his snout up and down
my neck, while I squeal like a wench.
Any face seems drawn and long
in a casket, especially a face that looks
like your own face. Hold the leather
handles fast, brush the white patina rose
with the crease of your slacks.

In a room with coffee and cheese, a boy
is making himself a mourning plate.
Morning has broken is a hymnal line that means
two or more things. I realize this as I'm singing it,
the wafer crumbs still stuck inside my mouth.

Particulate Matter

At the bottom of a day, the heat begins,
its scent like dried thyme. A man holds
a rusted folding chair. This gesture:
he turns. Wind cuts the dirt yard,
kicks up a grayscale of lost winters.

Afternoon, and the flotsam and jetsam
of the summer garden, pale radishes
and encephalitic broccoli heads,
go who knows where. These rows
blister and burn themselves out.

In the dry creek bed, lusty crickets moan.
A man shouts an answer to the wind.
The planets dance on their axes,
brash, already spitting out degraded protons.

II.

In the spiral sky a taste like gods' sweat.
A man in a field holds a folding chair.
The chair is a face.
The face is on fire.
The fire is something I can't name,
a segment of memory
I turn away from, and turn,
until the whole field is on fire.

To the right of the man,
a mother holds a fistful of gnats,
tells me she is saving them for me.
Each gnat is a heartache I
can't remember.

III.

A man in a field holds a folding chair.
A deer sleeps in the grass, statuesque.
The man with the chair is my lover.

A father's father stands to his left.
His missing teeth are parallel universes.
At any moment they might collide and
nobody understands the nature of death.

IV.

A man in a field holds a folding chair.
His hair is made of light.
I realize I'm naked. He unfolds the chair and
sits down. When he opens his mouth,
horse flies fall out like a cataract.

They form the shape of a word: *HEY*

The History Of Yesterday

Origins have no location in this history:
a story of who did what, and when, and why.
The impetus could be orange blossoms, or cockatiels,
or a short story set in Texas; it doesn't matter.
All we have are fragments — the aluminum
melted under friction, and the paint, rust resistant,
left a burgundy splatter. A man named
one poem *Yesterday*, and one *Pussy Juice*.

School children fretted over spelling rules.
The zippers on their backpacks and jackets
broke as simultaneously as destructive orgasms.
Sometimes we remember the loud scream,
sometimes the loud scream remembers us.
Sometimes the sky is a dirty slut, sucking off the sun.

For Posterity

Each, by their own degree, electrically
setting off Eden. Each Adamic afterthought.

Each ethos. Each interview. Scourge
of the new socks, scour the shirt collar.

A crêpery of creases. Crevice filled with sweat.
Do don't ask permission. To be a woman,

something slightly less frazzled. How eclectic.
How morning-dew. How I've forgotten

the chirp of the cricket, the plaintive
slide of limb on exoskeleton. Even there

image surrounds idea, I said, Go publish
a bird's nest. I said, Poe lived in many

empty houses. A drop of ink resembles
a raven, always leaving the window frame,

aloft and pregnant with metaphor.

Has Anyone Seen Autumn?

Has anyone seen autumn?
I made an appointment.
I read a book about pine trees.

Be a poor sport, nobody's looking.
Each day loaded with potential.
See the naked men and women with their faces cut out.

Dear Cartilage, You make hollow noises.
Thunder followed me south.

Formerly, I was all crickets and forgot to brush my dentines.
My mouth stunk.
Lullaby me.

Disintegrate me.
I told you about the first time I saw a penis.
(But I didn't tell you. You giggled.)

Cover your eyes and count my interior, observe
        its clovers and arrows.
I have a blue dress.

True north, like a mother/question, opened me up.
I can't take the flies away from your head.
Oh, leave me alone.

The Poem Is The Story (1)

Sometimes a story is like a beehive. Sometimes an idea
is like a poem. The common threat appears to be humanity,
but really it's gestalt. Or ennui. A woman slips
a microcosm up her skirt. Where'd it go?
Nobody knows, but what goes up must
come down, and so her underpants, stained with comet fire.
My best guess at the future is total annihilation
of the ego. To think is to string popcorn
on fishing wire and hang the finished product in a doorway.
I've mumbled an answer to an answer to an answer.
My reflection responded, cagey. This poem won't
have any nature imagery, unless it's used ironically,
like, The leaves of the trees whispered in the winkle, or,
A bird is a terrible thing to waste. I've always talked
this way, I say, you've just never noticed before. THE END

The Poem Is The Story (2)

The boy who moved to my town from California in sixth grade
made me a pair of earrings out of fishing wire and beads.
I threw them in the school trashcan at the end of the day,
and then years later felt horrible about it. That boy was just
trying to make a small gesture. Sometimes gestures
confuse themselves and seem more like questions.
One question is what is the answer. One question is how high
up does this ladder go, and if one were to fall from this height,
might one conceivably break bones? The poem is a collection
of objects, or of images. One can't always tell the difference.
The idea was to write something very quiet and subtle,
but then we were playing Oh Hell again at the kitchen table,
and out popped a poem with a curse word. THE END

The Poem Is The Story (3)

The funny thing to do now is to take a classic story
and retell it with caterpillars as all the main characters.
A protagonist is not the same as a proton, although both
eventually decay and spit matter back into the universe.
It's always good to know one dirty joke for cocktail parties.
The joke is better if it also makes fun of religion.
My friend has a great one that I can't put in this poem.
This poem could be a warm gray sweater in winter,
or it could be a box of condoms. I need one of those
things but not the other. This poem is almost certainly
constructed from letters and a confusion or profusion
of ideas, such as: One finds a train ticket on the sidewalk
and signals it and off one goes to Niagara Falls. That is a place
where weddings happen. The sound or the silence,
which is more distracting? The beehive. THE END

The Poem Is The Story (4)

Furthermore, the rate of decay is referred to as Red Balloon.
A kid sells cotton candy in bags at a busy stoplight in summer.
His face is like a handprint. His handprint is like a footprint.
His footprint is a valentine. I left a story in a story dangling
from a live oak in the Florida panhandle. What a waste.
Someone here is a giant asshole. Let's draw straws and see who.
It's probably me. In regards to car trips, I say yes.
In regards to the elderly being allowed to give their possessions away
willy-nilly after senility sets in, I say yes. In regards to tiger lilies, no.
The summer week without sun made my clothes smell better.
If I could just give the boy from sixth grade back his earrings
and say, Thanks, but no thanks, I would feel better.
Life is a series of such exchanges. Sometimes one performs well
and sometimes one is a total shit. Everyday the pattern
repeats. I left the book outside the door. THE END

The Poem Is The Story (5)

Red rover, red rover, send meaning on over. Send bubble-guns.
We will engage in a war of soap spheres. From where I sit
the frontierswomen are wide open, if you know what I mean.
Do you? Know what I mean? I mean I've struggled against
the hermetic lexicon long enough. I'll count to ten, but not
in this poem. This poem needs Kool-Aid. This poem needs
ketchup, or clowns. This poem is the story. A man
meets a woman. A problem happens. The problem resolves.
The man and the woman marry and have children.
They name one child after a misunderstanding
of identity in an old photograph. They name one
Mother-of-Pearl. An idea falls off the edge
of a countertop. This is the way the poem ends. THE END

Pasture

A man writes a poem about nature,
about a dead horse. This is a cliché.
The man has a square head.
In the poem something violent
happens and then the man has
an epiphany. This is formulaic.
What makes a poem not so?
In a smallish part of town,
one plants an idea. The idea stays
busy germinating. That is not
a poem. A woman and a man
step onto a city bus. The woman
almost falls in the walkway
when the bus jerks forward.
The man catches her. The man
is you. The woman is not me.
That is not a poem. A child strikes
matches and burns holes
in earthworms. The child has
an erection. He laughs. A handful
of loose words surround him.
That might be a poem.

Middle night, the glower of absence—
please, come into the room
where I don't have any poems left.